In Search of Truth

—Guru-Shishya Relationship

VISHAKHA CHANNA

First Published in March 2019

ISBN: 978-93-5347-279-5

BLUE ROSE PUBLISHERS

www.bluerosepublishers.com

info@bluerosepublishers.com

+91 8882 898 898

Cover Design:

Srijan Bandyopadhyay

Typographic Design:

Teena Maurya

Distributed by: Blue Rose, Amazon, Flipkart, Shopclues

Aapke Shabd Aapke Naam

Guru Bhramah, Guru Vishnu, Guru Devo Maheshwarah,
Guru Sakshat Parbhramah Tasmay Shri Guruveh Namah

He is…

He is an unsung hero of this land,
He silently battles for every man,
He does not care for caste or creed,
He comes charging on his steed,
When he hears a cry of need.

He is…

He is the tree that gives me shade,
He is the breeze of my changing fate,
He is the water of my needs,
He is the food that fulfils my needs,
He is the fire that keeps me warm,
He is my shelter from the storm,
He is the bulwark in my test,
He is the pillow on which I rest,
He is my life-giving rain,
He is the one to ease my pain,
He is my guide, so I cover miles,
He is the reason for my smiles,
He is my heart, he is my beat,
He is my hands, he is my feet,
He is the presence, he is the essence,
The sum total of my existence.
A thousand words cannot describe,

This rarest gem in my life,

A gem that shines ever so bright,

Yet very few see his light.

He is…

God’s gift to mankind.

CONTENTS

PREFACE

As a novice just about learning to crawl on the path of spirituality – it is rather presumptuous on my part to attempt to be the instrument through whom my Guru's words be put on paper, that too on a subject that the many adepts have waxed so eloquently about. That these words may serve as a beacon for those who wish to step off the bandwagon of what we call life and experience real life in all its hue and nuances even more so. The fact that the guiding light of these words is the Unknowable himself imbues confidence that those destined to benefit will do so.

A contradictory statement, yet those who have walked this path will agree. It is indeed a very difficult path to walk on and yet a very easy one. Difficult for those who hold onto their preconceived notions of living life, for we live in a hard-core materialistic world. Easy for those who are ready to give up these notions and take each step as a new way of living ones' life. The rules of living life remain the same – looking at them in a different light holds the key.

The book is divided into two parts. The first deals with my Guru's teachings and wisdom on the Guru-Shishya relationship.

The second gives the reader a very brief glimpse of my Guru. Brief, because he is the UNKNOWABLE and therefore, indescribable – words would not do justice to him. At best one can recount his physical existence on this physical plane. He is an experience that you experience.

INTRODUCTION

At the behest of my Guru, the following pages attempt to capture his wisdom, teachings and his guidance on the relationship between a Guru and his disciples. Teachings that he has imparted to all the aspirants who have been fortunate to have been blessed by his presence.

His wisdom and teachings are as ancient as the universe itself, but he has simplified them to the point of literally spelling out "A" for apple, "B" for ball… … … This he has done so for the human mind - to grasp and understand the complete essence in the current epoch of Kaliyug. If His wisdom and teachings were left in their pristine wordings, it would be akin to asking a crow to admire the beauty of a pearl.

The next few paragraphs are a digression from the topic but it would be worthwhile to take some time to reflect on your life lived so far, before you proceed any further. The reason for this digression is two- fold.

- to reiterate the obvious for those who have actively searched for a Guru and having found one feel overwhelmed by circumstances that arise and thus need stepping stones to guide their steps in their relationship with the Guru.

- to draw a background for those who have not actively sought a Guru out but find themselves in the presence of that Perfected Being who is ever willing to guide them. Such aspirants are equally at a loss as to the correct manner by which a Guru-Disciple relationship is conducted.

The premise in both the cases being that the aspirant is more interested in the spiritual progress than progress in the material world.

Most of you would have spent the early years of your life getting an education. For those geeky nerdy ones, those years would have been a pleasure. For those not so inclined towards studies, maybe not. Whatever may have been your inclination, your life would have had its share of highs and lows. Knowing that you had something to look forward to at the end of your education – namely your career – was enough of an impetus to overlook the lows and celebrate the highs.

You embarked on your life journey with great enthusiasm for you felt that you were in control of your life. There were goals to be achieved, inventions and discoveries to be made, new theories to be propounded, businesses to be built, wrongs in the world to be set right. Whatever may have been the path which you set out on, there was a sense of purpose. Some of you would have trailblazed your way to the pinnacles of success, fame would have courted some, success would have eluded some, others would have slowly and steadily gone about their careers and for some their dreams would have shattered.

In this milieu of education and life's journey you also had to deal with human beings. Family, friends, colleagues, acquaintances, the not so friendly people – relationships did blossom, and they did wither - enriching your life and its experiences. All in all - life has been fairly satisfactory, if not good to you. You most probably have the basic creature comforts that make life worth the while as the average man knows it to be. Some of you probably live in the lap of luxury and think life could not be better. Yes, some of you would have had more than your fair share of trials and tribulations, and for you, life maybe nothing but an uphill task, a drudgery that needs to be dealt with.

Good or bad, however life may have treated you, a general air of dissatisfaction gnaws at you. You are in quest of that something in life that you have not experienced so far. A missing link that you cannot pinpoint. If life has been good to you – you have probably not found the key to internal peace and happiness. If it has not – then you are searching for an answer to a question that has dogged your every step – why me? You may belong to neither of the above categories but to that minority who have taken in their stride what life has thrown at them – good, bad, indifferent. If this book is in your hand, you are probably searching for that one thing that can show you the true meaning of life. Whatever be your take on life you were provided with the wherewithal that helped you in your journey, so far.

To all the physical and psychological aspects of life, we make it interesting by adding another facet. The facet called religion. Whether we actively practise or not the tenets of the religion we are born into, proves to be a small but a very decisive factor of life. Small, because in the pursuit of life, for majority of us, it is just that – small. Our busy schedules and chock-a-block diaries hardly ever have prayers penned into them. We arrange our prayers (if at all) to fit into our life's schedule. It hardly ever strikes us to make a schedule for our prayers and arrange our life around it.

We use our religion and prayers as a security blanket, as a crutch. They are supposed to help us fulfil our material wants, be it a better job, a bigger car, a larger house, pots and pots of cash, success for our children etc. A prayer answered, finds our faith in our religion growing in leaps and bounds. On the other hand, an unanswered prayer finds our faith on a shaky wicket. We run around priests, pandits, astrologers, maulvis and their ilk, hoping to find the right formula to crack the code to our difficulties. It could be undertaking a pilgrimage, visiting a dargah, counting a rosary, wearing a cross/lucky charm – anything that helps us. Our religion and prayers are just a means to fulfil our worldly desires.

For a handful of us religion plays a decisive role. We feel the need to commune on a day-to-day basis with the one to whom we address our prayers to. It matters not, if a prayer is answered or not. The belief is strong enough to trigger a need to look beyond the prayers, the rites and rituals, the do's and don'ts that our religion entails. The belief urges us to walk up to that doorway that may give us a glimpse of that world that seems to lie entrapped in the tombs written by the Vivekanandas and Rumis of this world. What or who is the doorway, one may ask? The answer is – The Guru – he is the doorway, the journey and the goal that you seek.

In a world filled with countless Godmen and Men of God whose actions tend to break rather than make your faith – the search for a true Guru is indeed a very difficult search. In the current world scenario where violence in the name of religion marks every corner of the globe, material acquisitions is equated to the greatness of a man, selfishness and corruption is rampant and the many ills that plague our society, we are hardwired sceptics. It is through this lens that we view and judge, and should we be presented with the opportunity to meet a perfected being, very often fail to recognize him.

Very few amongst us are lucky enough to find a true Guru. If indeed, you are the fortunate one to have found that Perfected Being then the words that follow may just be the beacon that lights the path of your journey with him.

PART-1

SEARCH FOR A GURU

Circumstances in our lives are an outward manifestation, the tangible aspect, that provides us with the impetus to start our search. This alone is not enough. Your Guru shall not suddenly appear at your doorstep and neither will you find your way to his. There is another aspect, the intangible, i.e. the inner impetus. How strong a desire you have clearly dictates the probability of you being able to find your Guru. Which path you choose to fuel this desire is an individual choice. It could be meditation, counting the beads, undertaking pilgrimages, reading scriptures, visiting seers and savants, participating in communal prayers etc. Then again desire is not enough. It needs to be backed by your belief and faith. You believe and have faith that what you are doing is the way forward and you have faith that you will achieve the desired result, sooner or later.

A little digression again. We must not confuse belief with faith and vice versa. We often think of our belief as our faith. That is not the case. Belief is something that produces results which we can measure. Winds of change very often undermine our beliefs and we find that our beliefs do take wings too. We often dither in our beliefs and what better illustrates this point than this short true life-story -

A householder firmly believed in the tenets of the religion he was born into and assiduously performed all the rituals and prayers required of him. He was blessed with two sons and with passage of time the family grew to include grandchildren. Tragedy struck, he lost one of his sons. Overnight anything to do with prayers and rituals was shunned. ***This is belief.***

Whereas, faith is an absolute conviction that is there to stay – a steadfast friend. It holds steady in the face of adversity. You cling to it for your dear life, knowing that the storm shall pass, and calm shall return. It stands a vanguard against changing winds, as it did for this believer -

A householder firmly believed in the tenets of the religion she was born into. She led a blessed family life, being sincere in her religious duties. A time came when she lost three members of her family in a span eight months. Her beliefs were not shaken, she continued to be as committed to them as she had been before tragedy struck. ***This is faith.***

It is this faith, that you need to stoke to such a fevered pitch that it carves a gaping hole in your heart and mind that only the presence of a Guru can heal. It compels nature to work towards grafting a path to the Guru's doorstep or the Guru calls out to you for he knows you, the human vessel is receptive and willing to follow the Guru. If your Guru has come calling for you, then it is almost a given that He is the one for you – intuitively you feel it in the depths of your heart. He holds you spell bound, enamoured by the grace and love that just seems to ooze out of his very being. When you are not in his presence the urge to re-establish a connection with Him is so strong that the feeling is akin to that of gasping for breath and knowing that your existence depends on your very next breath.

However, if you have reached his doorstep through your efforts, how do you know He is the one for you? After all, you know nothing about him. You may know his name, may have heard about him. But other than that, nothing. Well, it is a very intuitive process. It is not the tangibles i.e., what he says or does that clinches the so-called deal for you. It is how he makes you feel. There is an attraction, or should one say a magnetism that pulls you towards him. You may resist it, but sooner or later you find yourself gravitating towards him. There is an inexplicable sense of inner peace that you experience in his presence. You come away from his company energized and with a sense of joy and wellbeing. A high that you want to experience again and again.

In either case, the underlying principles that will govern your relationship with your Guru can be summed up as:

a) Unflinching and unquestionable faith that you repose in your Guru.
b) Your sense of service and the true spirit and essence of your devotion to your Guru.
c) You make your Guru your highest priority – all actions and relations come after him.
d) Your open-mindedness to accepting your Guru's word as law, even when his words, against the canvas of life as you have known, seem confounding. Your willingness to integrate the same into your daily routine, while wondering about the practicality of it all given the vagaries of life.
e) The willingness to look at and accept your weaknesses and then bringing about a change in yourself.
f) Your willingness to shed all pre-conceived notions and unlearn all the knowledge that you have accumulated/acquired.
g) Carry the conviction that every adversity is a blessing in disguise.

h) Your journey is yours, so do not compare it with your fellow students.
i) Your acceptance of and attitude towards your Guru's family. By family – it does not mean just familial connections – it extends to your fellow disciples too.
j) Your Guru is the driving force in the relationship.
k) No matter what role your Guru decides to play in your life, be it that of a father, mother, friend, sibling – you are always only a student.
l) No matter how far in your journey your Guru may take you – you will ALWAYS sit a level lower than Him and will always be a step behind him. You will never know the true depth of your Guru.
m) Do not crowd the relationship with verbal cacophony.

These are not merely principles but stepping stones that can either break your back or forge it into steel. How you approach them is the essence. If, after reading the above you arrive at a conclusion that the hard work is all yours, then you are mistaken. You may as well bail out. The Guru's work is far harder than yours. You are just unaware of it. He takes on the responsibility of your karmic actions. Even those closest to your heart, your dearest ones, do not do that for you.

You, have to prove yourself to your Guru and convince him you are worthy of the honour he bestows on you by accepting you as his disciple. It's very similar to landing a new job. You are put on probation and only once you have proven your ability and capability to handle the job do you get confirmed.

TEST OF FAITH

Having reached your Guru's doorstep, you may just think that the toughest job is over. Do not fool yourself. The journey only gets tougher from here onwards; your mundane existence becomes easier. (Do not roll your eyes and think this is some esoteric jargon – the meaning of this sentence will become clearer as you read further on). It is not going to happen overnight – the easing of your life. As a matter of fact, in the initial phase you may wonder if you have pulled yourself out of the frying pan only to land in the fire. No, that is not the case.

You are probably exhausted with all your efforts searching for a Guru. His doorway for you is manna from heaven and you think you deserve a rest! Remember the foundation of faith you built before you undertook your journey? He is going to check the firmness/strength of that foundation. He wants to know how blind the faith that you have reposed in him is. In other words, the depth of your faith. You may ask what's wrong with your faith if it helped you find your Guru? Nothing. Your faith has not been tested against the tempest your Guru can unleash. He wishes to gauge the extent of your faith in your faith. The subtle difference between belief and faith has already been given. Examine this statement in that light – for if you truly understand this statement you have found the master key.

This initial test of faith usually involves the more material aspects of your life. It could be that you suffer a severe financial loss, you are beset with health problems or friends and family desert you. If you are wondering why these three aspects? The answer is simple – we associate life the most with these and attach a lot of importance to these.

In your spiritual journey, these are your first weaknesses that you have to overcome. It does not mean you have to do away with them. It just means that you need to look at them with the right perspective and accept them, without the urge to bring about a change in them to suit you.

At this point it would not be amiss to dwell on these aspects a little bit to understand how they work as impediments in your spiritual journey. Finance, health and relationships are the backbone of physical existence. You need money to cater to your requirements of food, clothes and a roof. Relationships form the support, infrastructure in your good times and bad times. Health contributes to the quality of life that you lead.

Your idea of the amount of money you need for your survival is not dictated just by your actual needs. It is dictated by numerous other factors, such as saving for a rainy day, reflection of your social status, inheritance that you would like to leave for the younger generation etc. In short, the fatter the bank balance, the safer you feel. Earning money is hard work. It claims a large chunk of your time and energy. The myriad activities that you need to perform in addition, to keep this bank balance at the safe levels that you deem to be right leaves you even more exhausted.

This pursuit of wealth leaves you with very little or no time or energy at all to reflect on the true nature of life.

Relationships again imbue you with a sense of safety. You feel you owe loyalty to those who have been there for you in both the good and bad times. There is nothing wrong with that loyalty per se. It proves to be an impediment when it blinds you to the true nature of the people with whom you have a relationship with. It is your refusal to accept them as they are that causes you unhappiness, and you feel they have let you down. Sometimes, your entire life seems to get derailed. A relationship that you can not view in an unbiased manner leaves you feeling divided between your commitment to them and to your spiritual needs and pursuits.

Good health – money stays in your bank and relationships stay intact. Bad health tests both – money of course finds its way to another's bank account. Relationships too get strained – for not everyone can take the pressure of caring for those in poor health or for that matter being able to carry on their day to day activities under reduced circumstances. Moreover, bad health also brings out the worst or the best in you. You truly realize your threshold to stay positive in the face of adversity and your ability to feed the fire of your search for the divine in adversity.

If you were riding a high in your life and are suddenly faced with all possible difficulties – the thought that these difficulties have come visiting you only after the advent of your Guru in your life, is bound to arise. If life was cruising along, it was neither good nor bad, then, again, this thought will arise. If you were head over heels in trouble and your difficulties only seem to compound, you are bound to ask, what the heck has happened? Just put your head down and continue to do your best to overcome your difficulties. Through these difficulties your Guru is teaching you to understand that your needs and wants are not the same.

Moreover, he is opening your eyes to the fact that what you want is not necessarily good for you, even if you think that is the case.

These are passing storms to test the faith you have reposed in your Guru. You do not have a clue, he is holding your hand – he will not let you fall. He whispers words of encouragement, assures you your troubles will end. Do not mistake them to be words meant to placate you. These are his promises and his way of providing you the light in your times of trouble. Let his words continue to be the oil that lights the lamp of your faith. He will push you to the brink, wherein you feel the walls are closing onto you. At this critical juncture if you are going to rave and rant, let doubts creep in, loose your mental equilibrium – you have just made matters worse. Your moments of agony will prolong themselves. You may ask why? The answer is that doubts cannot co-exist with faith just as day and night cannot exist in the same moment of time.

It is just not the strength of your faith that he is testing, it is the strength of your character too. He knows you better than you know yourself. So, why does he need to do it? Ah! It is his compassion for you. He is giving you the oppotunity to face your weaknesses. He is giving you the free will to choose. You can either accept and overcome your weaknesses and begin the process of uprooting them out of your personality, or you can dig in your heels, and not acknowledge the same and thereby, loose the game.

Your faith will be tested time and again. This initial test is more for your benefit than for your Guru's. It gives you a good glimpse of the hardships you will face and whether you would want to continue the journey. It is the first distillation, separating the wheat from the chaff. You will either be a follower or a disciple. A Guru may have many followers, but his disciples are always few.

Once your Guru accepts you as his disciple, your faith will be tested to a breaking point – a stage further along in your journey. The severity of the test depends on how far along you are on the spiritual path and at what point your spiritual journey will end in this lifetime. A story related to this that portrays this amply and succinctly.

A guru once decided to put his followers to a test. When the time for prayers came, he set out for the place of worship as did those gathered around him. They followed him as he started walking but were puzzled when they realized that the Guru was taking a different route than the usual. Nonetheless, they continued to walk with him. As the time for prayers approached nearer, it dawned on them that they would not be in time for the prayers, for this indeed was a longer route. The so-called hangers-on decided to part ways. The Guru continued along his chosen route. The time for prayers crept nearer and nearer. One by one the followers started to part ways as they knew they would never be in time for the prayers. All but one deserted their Guru when they realized that the route chosen led them to the brothel house and not the place of worship. The lone follower followed his Guru. When the Guru entered the brothel house, he waited outside. Day turned to night, the disciple waited for the Guru to come out. The Guru stepped out only the next morning – the disciple was waiting for him.

That for you is a true disciple and true faith. That absolute conviction that the one and sole purpose of your life is to be with and to be of service to your Guru; for having realized God, your Guru represents and manifests the Divine Will on earth.

To sum up briefly as to why you need to be tested. When you come to your Guru's doorstep remember he welcomes you with open arms for he sees a potential in every human to grow spiritually and to reconnect with the divine. He gives you the opportunity to begin your journey. What you make of that opportunity and the journey thereof depends on your efforts and your ability to follow the rules of engagement of the Guru-Shishya relationship

A FOOTNOTE TO THE TEST OF FAITH

You may just be wondering what happens to your religious beliefs. Honestly, nothing. All religions are the same in the eyes of your Guru and he reiterates this point time and again. From your Guru's point of view – your present religion is an accoutrement that you shall give up at the end of this life. You have worn different ones in your past and will wear different ones in the future.

Your Guru will most definitely test your view on religious belief systems, i.e. your acceptance of all religions. Whether you have taken birth in the same religion as your Guru or not, it is of little consequence. He could ask you to visit a place of worship that may not represent your religion, he may ask you to recite a prayer that is not from your prayer book or he may ask you to either start observing or stop observing some or all rituals.

Religion is just a vehicle/tool in your journey to begin to understand the Absolute. The rites and rituals and the dos and don'ts are just visual perceptible aids, that you, as a layman need, to familiarize yourself with the abstract concept of the Absolute. As you progress along this path, a point comes when you transcend the need for these aids. It is at this point that you realize that at the heart all religions lies buried the kernel of spirituality. In other words, spirituality is the source or fountainhead of all religions.

He will never ever ask you to change your religion. Equally if the rules of your religion are contrary to those of his – the rules of engagement of your religion will be respected in equal measure. This may sound contradictory (in a layman's eyes), however, it is the truth.

THE JOURNEY BEGINS

Your journey truly begins only after you have been granted entry into your Guru's doorway. You have now been accepted as a follower. (You may think otherwise, but that is of no consequence.) There will be those who have come before you and there will be those who will come after you. Your journey with your Guru will travel on its own trajectory – do not compare it with that of your fellow followers. Your Guru knows your destiny just as he knows the destiny of every other soul that darkens his doorway and the potential of his followers. He works very closely with not only those who are destined to be granted discipleship, but also with those who show a great potential but may fall on the wayside sooner or later. This falling off, of the aspirant is either due to the aspirant's faith not having deep enough roots or the aspirant's unwillingness to put his or her ego on the backburner to bring about a change in himself/herself. The aspirant is invariably looking at and judging the Guru as he or she would an ordinary human being.

A quick flowchart to give you a bird's eye view of what this journey entails before any explanations are put forth.

GURU'S GUIDANCE

To help the disciple understand

LIFE = BALANCE SHEET OF KARMA

What constitutes karmas & What needs purification

KARMA (YOUR DEEDS OF ACTION, SPEECH AND THOUGHT)

How to purify your karma

BY BECOMING MINDFUL OF YOUR KARMAS

How to become mindful

BY ACCEPTING AND UPROOTING YOUR WEAKNESSES

How to uproot your weaknesses

BY BECOMING AWARE OF YOURSELF

How to become aware of yourself

BY UPROOTING YOUR WEAKNESSES

This uprooting leads the disciple to understand

WHAT CONSTITUTES BAD AND GOOD KARMA

Understanding the nature of karma

THE DISICPLE UNDERSTANDS THAT LIFE IS A BALANCE SHEET OF KARMA

THIS UNDERSTANDING HAS BEEN POSSIBLE ONLY DUE TO YOUR GURU'S GUIDANCE

The above chart is just to help you understand the things you need to be mindful off in the journey that you undertake. No action is mutually exclusive of the other. You need to train your thinking process to bring about a cohesion of the various points made above to succeed in your endeavours. Overlooking of a single aspect will make your journey a harder one.

Your Guru starts the process of cleansing and purifying you, the disciple. Your Guru takes on the responsibility of cleansing your Karmas – he wipes clean the slate of Karmas that you have accumulated, since birth. These karmas are karmas of action, thought and speech. He willingly takes on the burden of your karmas and works them out through his physical body – this usually manifests itself as a sudden illness – for his physical body is subject to the limitations of this physical plane. You can now write afresh on this slate which he has cleansed for you.

It is imperative that you keep a vigil over your actions, speech and thought. Every time you commit a mistake i.e. your karmas have a negative fall out - your Guru bears the burden. The fact that the first thing that your Guru did was to wipe off all your negative karmas from your slate, changing the very balance of your balance sheet of karmas, tells you how important it is to be mindful of what you do, say and think. In your mind, actions performed is equivalent to a karma. In your life you give some importance to your speech (for others hear it and thereby react) but never to your thoughts. You believe that your thoughts being hidden from the scrutiny of others do not reflect on your karmas. That is a mistake you need to rectify. For an outwardly good deed having birth in negative emotions does not constitute a good deed in the karma balance sheet. You look at life as a sum of relationships and achievements but not as a sum of karmas that you have carried over from a previous lifetime, karmas you have accumulated in this lifetime, or will carry over to the next lifetime.

So, how can you be mindful of your karma? It is possible to do so by being aware of yourself. This is the purification process, that is your responsibility as a disciple. You can only be aware of yourself if you accept your character flaws and make a sincere effort to overcome them. This helps you to be an observer in any given situation. You can act in accordance to what a situation demands and prevent yourself from reacting. This control over yourself is a way to perform a karma that is in accordance with the spiritual laws. Let us analyse a situation to help us understand this better.

A Guru is sitting with his disciples and he reprimands one of his disciples for not having control over his anger. The disciple reacts – he feels the need to justify himself and his voice carries anger. The Guru just smiles and lets things pass. Sometime later the Guru once again reprimands the same disciple. This time he acts. He halts the spark of irritation/anger, apologises for and acknowledges his mistake and assures the Guru that he would be more mindful.

In the first instance, he has created a whole lot of negativity – a bad karma – the burden of which falls on his Guru's shoulders. The Guru's love and compassion is so intense, that he willingly takes it on, forgives the disciple, wipes clean the karmic slate for the disciple to re-write on. In the second instance, the disciple had worked on himself and, therefore, he was able to halt that spark of irritation/anger. On the balance sheet of karmas he stopped a bad karma – the burden of which would have been borne by his Guru. So indirectly he was able to serve his Guru by not adding to his burdens. He apologized and acknowledged his mistake – he is accepting of his weaknesses - he was able to keep his ego (a cause of many a bad karmas) on the backburner. His assurance equates to the fact that he is becoming more aware of himself – he is realizing how he must conduct himself in any given situation.

There is yet another fact that you need to be mindful of. Just because your Guru has reprimanded another disciple and not you, does not mean that you do not have to be careful. It could also be an indirect manner of warning you and the other disciples that some amongst the gathering too need to work on this issue. This indirect reprimand may be because you or the other disciples have not been able to master this aspect of your personality well enough and may have reacted as that particular disciple had done in the first instance. This indirect reprimand is also the Guru's way of showing you how to conduct yourself in a situation that can cause another to react and thereby commit a mistake. Another lesson that you take away from this experience is how actions and reactions influence another human being's life – how they effect others' balance sheet of life just as they do yours.

Your Guru's presence itself produces an environment that is conducive to help you maintain self- awareness at higher levels. But how do you pursue these higher levels in your daily life – an amalgamation of relationships, emotions and activities within and outside the family circle. How do you learn to weave the warp of your spiritual journey with the weft of your life journey that is bound by the physical and social norms? In other words, how do you integrate your Guru's teaching in your day to day life? The answer is by making your Guru your top priority. Let us take another example and analyse it:

At your place of work, you are due for a promotion and you have worked hard to ensure that you get it. You do get it. In normal circumstances, how are you likely to respond? You are likely to be overcome by a sense of self-importance and pride and your thoughts will probably be "I deserved it". If you make your Guru your top most priority then:

a) *Your initial response may be that you experience a sense of pride that your hard work paid, but then you check yourself, send a prayer of thanks to your Guru and accept good wishes with humility – means you are working on raising your level of self-awareness, integrating your Guru's words in your daily life but still need to work on yourself where your first thought will be that of your Guru.*
b) *You send a quick prayer of thanks to your Guru, understand it as a blessing from Him – there is a sense of satisfaction and may be pride (depending on how far into the journey you are) in what you have done – means that you are becoming self-aware in an environment that may not necessarily promote it, you are integrating your Guru's words in your daily life, you also understand the interplay of your karmas on other's live - for had you allowed yourself to experience a sense of pride instead of satisfaction – your Guru would have had to carry the burden of negativity created by pride.*

In all of this you are simultaneously uprooting your flaws surely but steadily.

While we are all aware of what constitute human flaws, it would not be amiss to reiterate them. Anger, Greed, Desire, Pride and Ego are the stumbling blocks that impede your spiritual journey. More often than not, you do not recognize them for what they are because in your day-to-day existence you can always justify them. You lost your temper or made an error of judgement because somebody said something or caused it to happen. You need more wealth and power because others equate them with greater respect and higher social status. In your eyes the root cause lies outside of yourself and, that in your eyes is a justification by itself.

You do not consider your ordinary daily actions as a balance sheet of karmas. Therein lies the secret of the beginnings of being aware of yourself. However, your spiritual journey is an inward journey – all root causes lie within you.

A good way to overcome your weaknesses is to train your mind to look at the larger picture and where you stand in that picture. An example my Guru often gives that puts things in a great perspective.

The chef is complemented for producing a delicious meal by one and all who partake of it. The natural outcome of all the praise is that the Chef experiences a sense of pride at his achievement. Now, if the chef was to look at the larger picture, it would go something like this. The chef would not have been able to produce the meal had it not been for the help he received from his co-workers or if he had not had the necessary ingredients. The ingredients that he needed were produced by someone other than himself. In between the producer and the achiever, i.e. the chef, there were a million others involved – those who harvested, processed and transported the ingredients, the transportation was possible because someone else manufactured the mode of transportation. Add to this the person who filled fuel into the vehicle, the fuel came from elsewhere, where there were many who helped in the process of extracting the fuel, so on and so forth. The praise that the chef got was possible only because nameless faces and endless hands contributed towards the result.

When you look at this larger picture you realize that you are just a mote of dust in the vast landscape of human existence. Pride and ego will naturally take a backseat. Lo and behold you have taken a step closer towards uprooting your flaws. Overcoming your flaws and uprooting them from your being does not happen overnight. It is an ongoing process. Your Guru is always looking for the sincerity with which you work on yourself. While you may think you are doing all the hard work, he is fine tuning your thought process behind the scenes to help you overcome your weaknesses – you will be completely unaware of this. You have begun to master your flaws when in any situation – good or bad – you find yourself more at peace and accepting of the outcome.

THE JOURNEY CONTINUES

Let us answer a few questions that may have arisen in your mind after having read what you have.

Why does each disciple's journey travel on its own trajectory? After all the goals (spiritual) are common! Would not a comparison put things in the right perspective, especially when not many travel on this path?

The answer is very simple – your karmas are not the same as another's. You have no clue of the number of lifetimes you have lived or for that matter of the carry forward of your past lifetimes that you are dealing with in the present lifetime. Neither did you, before you met your Guru even look at your life as a balance sheet of karma – so you have no idea of what you have accumulated in this lifetime. Neither are you aware of how far you have walked on this spiritual path in your previous lifetimes or what halted your progress, or did you simply run out of time in your previous lifetimes. Your Guru not only knows your every lifetime, your spiritual progress and every karma but He also knows your strengths and weaknesses and your character traits like the back of his hand. He can, and therefore does, chalk out your spiritual journey accordingly. This dictates your experiences of the intangible, while the goal posts remain the same for all. The intangible cannot be compared.

Does the purification process stop?

Not really. It is an ongoing process as long as you are travelling on this road. Your degree of self-awareness increases the longer you are on this road. This self-awareness leads you to self-control (you act consciously) that helps you to mitigate your mistakes. It does not mean you can let your guard down. For letting down your guard will allow ego to walk right back in and impede the purification process.

To be aware of yourself you need to remove your flaws and to remove your flaws you need to be aware of yourself! A little bit like the chick and the egg story! What comes first?

These two processes are entwined – one leads to the other and vis-a-versa. Your Guru holds up a mirror to you for you to come face to face with your weaknesses. He may initially even point them out in plain simple language and ask you to work on them so that they are not an impediment to your spiritual progress. It could be, He asks you to love more or tells you your familial attachments are in the excess or that money is the driving force of your life etc. It is akin to making you realize that your car is tanked up (your flaws are part of you and he holds the mirror for you), the key is in your hand (he makes you aware of them and tells you what you need to do) and all you need to do is put the key into the ignition if you wish to start the car (the process of purification of self is then in your hands). Your Guru has kick started the awareness process and then leaves it to your free will to let the process gather speed and reach its natural end.

The physical hard work is yours, so why can you not take the credit?

You get the credit in the eyes of the world. No one asks you about behind the scene workings. Look at the larger picture. Is the credit all yours? Your hard work paid off because of the help from quarters you reached out to and some from those you did not. The most important factor is that the blessings were with you. The sceptics may call it luck. What is luck – if not blessings of the Unknowable and help from the Unknown. As was said right in the beginning – rules of living remain the same, looking at them from a different perspective holds the key.

YOUR GURU TAKES PRECEDENCE OVER EVERYONE AND EVERYTHING

You may just ask, Why? But, Why not?

Does he not take on the onus of changing the very the balance of your karmic sheet in your favour?

You set out in search of your Guru because a certain sense of dissatisfaction in your daily life gnawed at you. Had you been capable enough of finding an answer to your dissatisfaction, you would never have set out searching for a Guru. So, having found one, you now understand that your Guru is the doorway, the journey and the goal. You have found the doorway i.e. your Guru. You have started your journey i.e. your Guru has accepted you as his disciple. How to you get to your goal – by focusing solely on the goal i.e., your Guru.

If you were to cast your eye to the ordinary mundane world, you realize that each of us focus on an aspect that is of prime importance to us. For a householder it would be looking after his family, for a mother it would be her infant, for the career-oriented it would be his/her job, for the one wanting to amass wealth all efforts would be directed accordingly, so on and so forth.

Similarly, on the spiritual path your Guru is of prime importance. Your ability to give priority to your Guru over everyone and everything is in direct proportion to the strength and intensity of your burning love and desire to be with your Guru and your willingness to feed this fire. Initially in your journey you may find it difficult but if you make a concerted effort you realize that focusing solely on your Guru helps in other spheres of your life too.

The moment you make him the centre of your universe, your ego takes a back seat. You find it easier to raise your levels of self-awareness. It, therefore, becomes easier to overcome and uproot your weaknesses. Humility becomes second nature to you for when ego takes a back seat the idea of "I" loses its hold on you and a natural realization dawns that your existence is the result of the divine will. The divine will that is manifested through your Guru on this physical plane.

How you go about achieving this sole focus is individually driven. The question worth asking yourself at this point of time is will your lifestyle and commitments dictate the precedence that you accord to your Guru or will the precedence that you accord to your Guru dictate your lifestyle and commitments?

RULE OF ENGAGEMENT

You are a disciple/student and a disciple/student you shall remain throughout your journey with your Guru and this is the simple rule of engagement that you need to keep in mind. No matter, how adept a student you may become, your Guru is always miles ahead of you. He has already completed his journey – he is there for your benefit to provide you the requisite guidance.

Your Guru understands you better than you do yourself and he knows what role to play in your life to bring out the best and the highest possibility from a spiritual standpoint in you. So, He may play the role of a parent, a friend, a sibling, a confidante, a teacher, it could be anyone. No matter what role he chooses to play, you always need to remember that you are a student. Being a student defines the limitations within which you need to conduct yourself – not only with your Guru but also with his immediate family. The reasons are two-fold:

a) As a student, your mind intuitively builds invisible checks and balances as to the right and wrong way of doing something. You know that as a student you need to be mindful of the language you use and of the liberties you take with your Guru and this, then naturally lends itself to your interaction with his immediate family. If you cast your mind back to your childhood days, it is not difficult to recall your behaviour – only difference is that you may have been able to hoodwink your school teachers with your false sincerity, but you cannot do so with your Guru. There are no half measures with him – he has already shown you the mirror.

b) As a student you are not ashamed to say, "I do not know"– opening yourself to the possibility of immense learning and of inculcating humility. This realisation and acknowledgement, of not knowing, naturally tempers down a sense of arrogance or intellectual superiority. This tempering, paves way to a lesser likelihood of any transgressions that could prove to be an impediment to your spiritual journey.

You are wondering why when your Guru has accepted you as his daughter or son (and he proclaims it openly), should your relationship with him be limited to that of a student?

The answer is very simple. Look back on your life and you will find that somewhere along the line, as parents you have pandered to your children's ego and as children you have expected your parents to pander to your ego. It is with this notion that you look at your Guru when he calls you a son or a daughter. When your Guru's behaviour is contrary you stand in judgement and this leads to a breakdown of your relationship.

On the other hand, a teacher who wanted you to learn well had no qualms in letting you know where you stood with him – irrespective of your IQ levels. You were left with no option but to put aside all your expectations and notions of what a teacher should be like or the nature of the subject matter to be learnt. You shed your preconceived notions and therefore you learnt. You understood that you were a student and that you were with your teacher to learn – ***YOU LEARNT.***

You searched for a Guru, for you thought that there was more to life than what you had experienced so far. You wanted to know more – i.e. you needed to learn something that would help you lead a more meaningful life. If you wish to learn, you need to be a student and for you to succeed you need to remain a student.

Your Guru does not differentiate between anyone. You are his family but remember he has a very large family. He treats everyone, even a stranger (in your eyes, not in his), as one of his own. Therefore, it only stands to reason that you set your boundaries so that your relationship does not come in conflict with other's needs and their relationship with him. If you feel that you are the centre of his universe, so do the others – for he does not differentiate. They are as entitled to his time and attention, as you are. Therefore, is it fair that you take up all his time and attention? Are you mindful of how your behaviour affects others?

In todays' day and age when commuting and communicating is child's play – do you not need to be mindful of the time that you choose to contact your Guru? After all, He is subject to the physical limitations of this physical plane. He too gets tired, He too falls ill, He too needs time to himself and time for his immediate family.

Your Guru is not here on this earth for your earthly gratifications. He has far greater responsibilities – He manifests God's will on earth. Therefore, are you justified in diverting his energies away from the bigger issues that face mankind? It bodes well to bear in mind, that he knows everything concerning you – even the most mundane things that you do not even give a thought to. Therefore, even without your communicating every single detail to him, He will direct you in the right direction, in the right manner, at the right time. It is imperative that you do not crowd your relationship with him with verbal cacophony – you may miss out on learning how to communicate with him in your heart and with his heart – you are a student in the school of spiritual sciences and not social sciences.

There is a lot to learn from his silence and from his interactions with others. A story retold, another's grievance addressed, encouragement to yet another can be an answer to your own doubts and questions even when not worded.

THE DRIVING FORCE

This Guru-Shishya relationship harks back to the 14th century, in India and beautifully exemplifies the respect and regard that the Guru and the Disciple had for one another and yet the student never forgot that she was a student and her Guru, the driving force of their relationship.

A Guru one day decided to play a game of hide and seek with his disciple. He asked his disciple to hide so that he could then find her. The student whose spiritual attainments were almost at par with her Guru's was thrilled to play the game with her Guru. She hid and called out to her Guru to find her. Her Guru sought her across the seven seas, across the seven heavens, in every possible corner of the universe, but to no avail. He admitted defeat at not being able to find her and asked her to come out of hiding. When she did, he asked her, where had she stayed hidden for so long. She revealed that she had hidden herself in the stone embedded in the ring that he wore, acknowledging that were it not for his inspiration she would not have known where to hide.

If the afore mentioned story does not convince you to give up the reins of your life to your Guru. Maybe this just may. This incidence goes back only a few years ago. On meeting his Guru for the first time, the first few words that the disciple was told by his to be Guru were that he was born because his grandmother wished for his birth. It was so true. His grandmother had indeed requested her guru to bless the disciple's parents with a child (the couple until then had not been blessed with a child) – the disciple being the result of that request.

Your Guru is the driving force of the relationship between him and you. If you must ask why, then the answer is - your Guru has already completed his spiritual journey. He is a God realized Perfected Soul, who in the human form, subject to the limitations of the physical plane, is on this physical plane for the benefit of his disciples and mankind at large.

Having realized God, he knows how arduous a journey it is and the pitfalls that a human being faces. He also knows that fine tuning your physiology is as important as purifying your soul, to help you handle the Universal Energy. Being a Perfected Soul, he knows how to handle God's energy. He works as a conduit that tempers' God's energy so that you may be able to handle it without coming to harm. There have been adepts who have achieved their highest spiritual possibility without the guidance of a Guru, but they have paid a very heavy price teetering between sanity and insanity, before finding their balance.

Moreover, your Guru knows your past, present and future, your strengths and weaknesses. He also knows how evolved a soul you are, and where your spiritual pursuit will end in this lifetime. He accordingly steers you through a course that he charts so that you are open to and can achieve (entirely dependent on your efforts) the highest possibility in your spiritual pursuits.

It does not mean that he bulldozes his way with you. As a matter of fact, he is ever willing to hear your heart's desires. He is privy to your thoughts even before you are conscious of them rising in your mind. Therefore, he really does not need them verbalized. He does it more for your benefit, lest you feel he is bulldozing his agenda.

THE SPIRIT AND ESSENCE OF SERVICE

It is very difficult to explain what is meant by the true spirit and essence of service to your Guru. This spirit and essence rests solely on a disciple's depth of love for his Guru. A story may best express this.

This story goes back to the early 1900s. A renowned poet-saint, known more for his poems than for his spiritual attainments, had a midnight visitor. The visitor expressed his wish to have a glass of 'lassi'. The poet asked his servant to fetch some from the market. The servant was in a quandary – at so late an hour, where would he be able to procure a glass of 'lassi'. Nevertheless, he set out to procure one. He had barely gone a few hundred yards, the sight he saw baffled him. At the corner of the street, a shop was selling lassi. He had never seen this shop before. The shopkeeper sold the glass of lassi at no cost saying that "this give and take continues between him and me". The servant quickly took the glass back for the visitor. His curiosity had been peeked. He decided to follow the visitor when he took leave. What he saw had him completely flummoxed. One moment the visitor was crossing the threshold of the house and the next moment he was at the corner of the street and with the next stride he had vanished. At the same time, he noticed the shop at the corner of the street too had vanished.

The servant asked the poet-saint who was the visitor. The poet-saint asked the servant to promise that during the poet's lifetime he would never reveal the identity of the visitor. After extracting the promise, the poet revealed that the visitor was none other than the saint Khwaja Moinuddin Chisti and the person selling the lassi was the saint Data Ganjbakhsh. The servant true to his master and his promise to him did not utter a word of this during the poet's lifetime. This incidence only came to light after the poet-saint had left for his heavenly abode.

GURU MA

Who is Guru Ma? She is the one who represents the feminine aspect of your Guru. To understand in earthly relationship terms, your Guru Ma could be, your Guru's mother, sister, wife, daughter or another lady disciple. Whatever be her relationship with your Guru and whatever be her age (earthly years), you need to accept her as your mother.

SHE IS…

How many roles does she fulfil?
A mother, daughter, a friend at will,
A wife, a doctor, a teacher too,
And a student to her Guru.

A silent sentinel she guards her lair,
Her beauty is beyond compare,
A watchful lioness, she protects her cubs,

Strikes those down, who dare to snub.

She straddles this world and the beyond,
Well aware, the chasm before her yawns,
The slightest slip can cause her fall,
She steps not back, but carries on.

Her wisdom belies her years,
The young and old, do her revere,
A pillar of strength for those who come,
The unseen scaffolding for the Silent One.

She warns her children of the rising tide,
Bears the brunt to ease their ride,
She lets them stay when the swell has died,
To learn and understand about life.

Her unstinted service to the Silent One,
Has Him a prisoner of her love,
He is the sun around whom she revolves,
She's his strength, he's her resolve.

She plays a very vital role not only in your Guru's life but also in yours. She understands your Guru better than anybody. She is his source of strength and so in complete tune with his moods, his needs, likes and dislikes that unwittingly she manifests His will. Your acceptance of her has to be at par with your acceptance of your Guru. The rules and principles of engagement of your relationship are the same as with your Guru. You need to accord her the same respect and the same reverence that you do to your Guru. There should be no difference in the spirit and nature of your service to her and that to your Guru. Your relationship with her is again defined by the limitations of your being a student.

A mother in the truest sense of the word – her large heart accepts every student as her own child. She dispenses love as well as reprimands in equal measure because she does not like to see her children fail in their endeavours. So, when you need a shoulder to cry on, she lends you the shoulder. When you need words of encouragement, she whole heartedly encourages you. If you need your ears to be boxed, be rest assured they will be. She will be in your corner batting hard for you with your Guru, if indeed you have won her love and confidence, which is no mean feat. In some ways winning her love is more difficult than winning your Guru's love.

You are unaware, but she too bears the burden of your karmas just like your Guru does. Of course, she never takes credit for it. For your misdeeds, she is at the receiving end of your Guru's wrath. It is, therefore, imperative that you are ever mindful of your conduct. She is generous with her love, advise and time for you and if you pay heed to her you will find your path is easier to tread on. This is so because her advise is so steeped in the practicality of life that you find it easier to integrate your Guru's teachings in your day to day dealings. She helps you understand your Guru's teachings when you find the going gets difficult. So, service to her, is service to your Guru. In the same vein, any disrespect towards her is disrespecting your Guru.

She has an unenvious role to play. She is both the buffer against your Guru and a conduit to him. As a result, she is looked upon as someone who curtails your access to your Guru. You need to understand that she only acts as a buffer either when she knows your Guru's workload is extremely heavy (not to say that it is ever light) and he needs the precious hours to fulfil the Divine Will or when she knows that the time is not right for you to receive an answer to your query (invariably on mundane matters) - in your mind's eye it may be a life and death situation – but in the larger picture not really. Her actions are guiding you to understand that silence is an integral part of your relationship with your Guru - not immediate gratification.

She is a conduit to your Guru – for understanding him the way she does and knowing the spiritual laws under which he operates, she has the unique privilege of giving you a glimpse of your Guru's true nature. The depth and magnitude of which is difficult for the human mind even to perceive. So, when spiritual laws prevent your Guru from telling you things, it is your Guru Ma who plays the role of young Krishna who opened his mouth for his mother Yashodha and gave her a glimpse of the entire world within him.

Your Guru and Guru Ma are halves of a whole to help you in your journey to the Divine.

P.S. Talking strictly from a worldly view point of gender sensitivity – if you are thinking why the female is in the background – there are females you are spiritually evolved and are gurus and their male counterparts represent the male aspect and play exactly the same role as your Guru Ma.

THE BEGINNINGS

My husband and I met our Guru in the August of 2014 and what a journey its been since then. Life has taken a 180 degree turn and definitely holds a different meaning for us. One understands the true nature of life, the true meaning of relationships better though it cannot be said that the understanding is complete. For on this path understanding that learning never stops, helps break the ego – the password to gain admittance into the spiritual world. One hopes and prays that just not the understanding and learning gains in depth, but that we can implement and integrate this understanding and learning in our daily lives.

Words are inadequate to express exactly what our Guru means to us or what he has done for us. Maybe this may give a glimpse of the difference our Guru's blessings have made in our life:

In my journeys far and wide,

My ship has seen its share of strife,

On the ever-changing tide,

My ship has blundered through the ride.

The storm came on stealthily feet,
Before long, my ship was meat,
It tried its best to find its feet,
But the storm kept up its beat.

In my darkest hour of need,
A gentle presence I did feel,
A presence I just had to heed,
And quietly followed in its lead.

My wrecked ship did he repair,
Sewed my sails with utmost care,
With gentle hands he steered around,
My ship in waters safe and sound.

He bears the burden of my cares,
Takes my pain, as if, it were his to bear,
Weeps the tears that are mine to shed,
Weathers storms that are mine to tread.

He is the wind that fills my sails,
The gentle wave that keeps me safe,
The star at night that guides my way,
The cherishing sun that warms my day.

And never does he once declare,

In your glory I have a share,

All he asks is for love and prayer,

So, God's blessings we all can share.

One can only hope and pray that we always find a place for ourselves at his feet and that our journey of discovery continues under his guidance and blessings.

PART-2

MY GURU

My Guru is a **living master** and does not wish that his identity be revealed. Suffice it to say that his spiritual heritage goes back to time immemorable.

My Guru was born on March 31st, 1952 in a royal family in the land of saints and savants. He was the only son of his parents. His father was a high-ranking government official. Keen that his son should lack for nothing in terms of worldly pleasures, receive the best in education and experience the world at large, he took my Guru with him - away from his mother and native place.

Of his father my Guru says. "He was a worldly creature for whom creature comforts and the give and take of relationships defined life. He had no spiritual inclinations and nor was he aware of my spiritual destiny at the time of my birth."

His mother was a very gentle, simple, large hearted lady. Of his mother my Guru says, "Her education was confined to the teachings of the Holy Quran which she knew by heart and could recite verbatim. She was in constant meditation."

My Guru lost his father at the tender age of 15 and his struggles in the physical world started thereafter. He says. "Till then I had led a very comfortable and a privileged life".

About himself, before he met his gurus, he says, "I was an ordinary man, not knowing what life was or what it meant? Life had meant living life like a prince, leading a luxurious life, eating the best of food and wearing the best of clothes."

His meeting with his first Guru was a bolt out of the blue. Whilst on a picnic with two friends, a stranger, guided them towards a spiritual adept. The adept was none other than **Sultan Sahib – my Guru's first Guru**. At that moment in time, my Guru was not aware of who the adept was or what lay ahead. Sultan Sahib, gave a pen to the first among the trio of friends – he is now a famous movie director. The second was given a newspaper – he is now a great versatile actor. To my Guru, Sultan Sahib gave water to drink – water that Sultan Sahib had used to wash his face. My Guru lost consciousness after drinking that water. When he regained consciousness, three days had elapsed, and he was a completely changed man. This was his initiation into the spiritual world. My Guru was around 19 or 20 years of age. Thereafter, nothing had greater importance for him than his Guru. He spent 17 years in the service of Sultan Sahib. However, it did not mean he lived a life of a renunciate. He held a full-time government job and fulfilled his familial commitments. It was his nights that he dedicated to his Guru. He led a simple ordinary life never allowing himself to be entrapped by the pride in his royal heritage.

Of his meeting with Sultan Sahib he says, "It was as if I had seen my soul. I was immensely attracted by him. A spring of love, affection and respect poured forth spontaneously".

Of his life with Sultan Sahib, my Guru says very little. All he says is that Sultan Sahib made him realize and understand the true nature of this world. He taught him that the only winner in life is love. He has been true to his Guru's teachings and has loved his fellow beings irrespective of their religion, caste, colour or creed to help them in their lives. He took to writing poetry and prose after he met Sultan Sahib. He has published books in his native language. Therefore, very few are familiar with his works.

Meeting with his second Guru was as unexpected as was his meeting with his first. In accordance with the tradition of his lineage, the designated day when monthly prayers were offered for the benefit of mankind came around. Due to his official commitments and the refusal by the officiating head of his department, to leave for home, my Guru was late for the prayers. He reached home to find the prayers already underway under the auspices of a saintly man – Sheikh Gulam Hassan. Sheikh Hassan's first words to my Guru were "You have been delayed for the prayers because the officiating head stopped you from leaving. Do not worry you will be the officiating head one day and you will run the show. I have been instructed to come and hold the prayers and guide you further in your spiritual journey."

Sheikh Gulam Hassan stayed with my Guru till he breathed his last in 1999 – a period of over 17 years.

About Sheikh Gulam Hassan, my Guru says, "He is the Master of Masters. He taught me how to balance the spiritual world with the materialistic physical world. He cleansed my soul of any dirt that was left and taught me the way of living in the world, as a common man for the service of mankind".

"It is he who guided me and taught me to cross the ocean of life without troubling anybody and to take the pain of the people and cure them with love. He has made the highest contribution after my first Guru in building my spiritual personality. He gave me the thought of humanity, love, affection and oneness, but during the 17 years he was putting my patience to test to see how much I can tolerate the ill will sent my way by others? How much I can resist the negative forces? How much spirits of nature I can digest and how much I can implement the rules of humanity?"

My Guru gives credit for everything in his life to his two Gurus. He says, "I was no one special – a soul unaware of its destiny. I was an ordinary man who incidentally met two great personalities; who built my behaviour, my conduct, my character and showed me realistic living (i.e. living in the world but not being of the world). I trusted my Gurus more than myself and had no doubts about anything. My Gurus were my boat. They were the oarsmen and the oars. I was witnessing the existence of the Creator in his Creation. I am blessed for it is in over a billion years that one does witness the creator and master in one. My only priority was my Guru and even now I do not have any aim except to be blessed by my Guru – that my beloved stays near me and I stay at his feet".

He says, "There are hundreds and thousands of miracles that I have witnessed of both my masters which are very difficult to explain to mankind at large. Only one incident that I would like to talk about – I had not taken permission from my Guru to attend Id celebrations with my family. On that day my Guru had told me 'Be with me'. But at midnight when physically my Guru was sleeping, I left his home and rushed back to mine. On my way to my residence I met with an accident. I remember my vehicle falling into a river and my driver and I drowning. My next memories are of waking up in the hospital without any major head injury.

Three months later when I met my Guru, I asked him as to whether he had come to save me. He replied that, at the time of the accident it was his hand that cushioned my head against the stone, and it was his hand that pulled me out of the river. Since I was unconscious and only regained it in the hospital, this memory had been wiped out. It was only when "Baba" mentioned this that I recalled being pulled out of the river by a holy saint in the dead of the night. Otherwise, at midnight, when I met with the accident there was nobody who could have saved me."

MY GURU'S BENEVOLENCE

In the chapter "Test of Faith" a statement was made "………your mundane existence becomes easier". Guru's benevolence makes this possible.

To help you understand this better, I am quoting a few incidences from the life of my Guru's followers. Before doing so, I need to make a clarification as to why the word mundane has been used. It is not to undermine the importance of the needs of day to day existence but to highlight the fact that until we were blessed by our Guru to see them in the correct perspective, for us they held a larger than life importance. Moreover, this perspective takes time to develop and it is our Guru's benevolence that helps by fulfilling our worldly desires.

There is no greater blessing than the birth of a child in the family. But what happens when this desire goes unfulfilled. We knock on heaven's i.e. my Guru's door. A childless couple came in the hope that their desire for a child be fulfilled. My Guru predicted a February pregnancy and exactly nine months from the day that he had predicted, they were blessed with their only child.

Some are blessed with the knowledge that they shall have the joy of seeing flowers bloom in their garden as was the case in the life of another follower. While the follower was still a bachelor, my Guru had told the follower a) the name of the girl he would marry b) he would be blessed with two sons and c) the names of his sons. The sonographer was blown out of his mind to have the test confirm what the follower already knew and that too twice over.

Parents' world shatters when they are faced with the mortality of their child. It was this pain that bought them to my Guru's doorstep. The child was suffering from cancer and had been given a very short time to live. My Guru cured him – it of course took a very heavy toll on my Guru's health. Today the child is on the threshold of adulthood.

The old embrace death so that they are released from their suffering, the young pray for the long life of their elders so that they may continue to bask in their love and protection. Two contrasting stories with the same end.

In one instance a young follower requested her Guru that her grandmother be blessed with a pain free long life. Her grandmother was in terrible pain as she was suffering from cancer. He told the follower her grandmother would live for another two and half years. Exactly after two and a half years her grandmother left her body.

While my Guru was sitting with his followers an unknown old couple came to him with an offering of sugar. My Guru lifted the old man's clothes with his stick and marked an area on his abdomen that was diseased and causing him tremendous pain and suffering. The old man's wife asked my Guru to release her husband from his suffering. My Guru asked the woman to use the sugar that she had brought for him (i.e. my guru) for making tea for her husband. He said that the man would be released from his suffering when the sugar finished. Two and a half days later when the last of the sugar was used up, the old man left his body – he was released from his sufferings.

For a person having familial responsibilities and financial commitments and no means to pay for those commitments, is a time of pure hell. In such a situation, your Guru blessing you with a job that literally comes walking to your doorstep is nothing but a miracle. This is the story of yet another follower.

A tale of siblings, one without a job and the other a victim of deceit. Today both are blessed – one has a job that is keeping her on her toes and the other has the court ruling in her favour (she had been asked to change her lawyer by my Guru, as unbeknown to her, he had been bribed by the other party) and is tying up the loose ends to keep the inheritance of her sons intact.

There is no end to my Guru's benevolence and endless reams can be written. At the same time all cannot be revealed, so one more instance of his benevolence before calling a halt to this narration. A follower was competing against 900 examinees. She requested her Guru to bless her with success in the examination. He asked her to work hard and told her that she would be in the top 20. She was 19th on the list.

There is no greater blessing for a follower than the assurance that his/her Guru's blessings will always be there through the ups and downs of life.

MY GURU'S MESSAGE

My Guru's teachings are encapsulated in this message for mankind:

"Life for me is only to serve mankind, nature's creation and that environment that protects the total planet. For me nobody is my enemy. I am a servant of the Creator and a servant of mankind and the creation of God.

Love all. Do good and be good to all for every human has within himself the Creator. Clear your negativity against your so-called enemies – it is your thoughts that perceive them so. Caste, colour, creed, religion are the perceptions and inventions of your mind. Your thoughts categorize things and people as good or bad, cleanse your thoughts.

Your religion is like the clothes you wear. You do not know what you wore in your past lifetimes and you'll exchange it for another in another lifetime. Therefore, respect all religions. Do not change your religion, change your thoughts.

To search for the Creator, search within yourself. The Creator exists within his Creation. In my school of philosophy there is no place for punishment or harshness. There is only love – with love every heart and every battle can be won. It is your Guru's love that removes all the internal dirt from you and saves you from negativity; which always exists within the human body and soul. It is his love that breaks your ego, removes the darkness from your soul and helps manifest self control. Only when your ego is truly broken can you gain entrance into the spiritual world. Once removed it automatically enlightens the human mind.

Life is too short for love, I wonder how people hate."

9 789353 472795

Printed by Libri Plureos GmbH in Hamburg,
Germany